Congressional
Research
Service

Agricultural Conservation:
A Guide to Programs

Megan Stubbs
Specialist in Agricultural Conservation and Natural Resources Policy

August 15, 2014

Congressional Research Service

7-5700

www.crs.gov

R40763

Summary

The Natural Resources Conservation Service (NRCS) and the Farm Service Agency (FSA) in the U.S. Department of Agriculture (USDA) currently administer close to 20 programs and subprograms that are directly or indirectly available to assist producers and landowners who wish to practice conservation on agricultural lands. The differences and number of these programs has created general confusion about the purpose, participation, and policies of the programs. While recent consolidation efforts removed some duplication, a large number of programs remain. The programs discussed in this report are as follows:

- Agricultural Conservation Easement Program (ACEP)
- Agricultural Management Assistance (AMA)
- Conservation Operations (CO); Conservation Technical Assistance (CTA)
- Conservation Reserve Program (CRP)
- CRP—Conservation Reserve Enhancement Program (CREP)
- CRP—Farmable Wetland Program
- Conservation Stewardship Program (CSP)
- Emergency Conservation Program (ECP)
- Emergency Forest Restoration Program (EFRP)
- Emergency Watershed Protection (EWP)
- Environmental Quality Incentives Program (EQIP)
- EQIP—Conservation Innovation Grants (CIG)
- Grassroots Source Water Protection Program
- Healthy Forests Reserve Program (HFRP)
- Regional Conservation Partnership Program (RCPP)
- Voluntary Public Access and Habitat Incentive Program
- Water Bank Program
- Watershed and Flood Prevention Operations
- Watershed Rehabilitation Program

This tabular presentation provides basic information covering each of the programs. In each case, a brief program description is followed by information on major amendments in the Agricultural Act of 2014 (P.L. 113-79, 2014 farm bill); national scope and availability; states with the greatest participation; the backlog of applications or other measures of continuing interest; program funding authority; FY2014 funding; FY2015 Administration budget request; FY2015 proposed funding where available; sequestration effects in FY2015; statutory authority; the authorization expiration date; and a link to the program's website.

Contents

Contacts

Introduction

The U.S. Department of Agriculture (USDA) administers a number of agricultural conservation programs that assist private landowners with natural resource concerns. These include working land programs, land retirement and easement programs, watershed programs, emergency programs, technical assistance, and other programs. The number and funding levels for agricultural conservation programs have steadily increased over the past 60 years. Early conservation efforts were focused on reducing high levels of soil erosion and providing water to agriculture in quantities and quality that enhanced farm production. Congress responded to these issues by creating and revising programs designed to reduce resource problems on the farm. By the early 1980s, however, concern was growing that these programs were not adequately dealing with environmental problems resulting from agricultural activities (especially off the farm). In 1985, conservation policy took a new direction when Congress passed the Food Security Act of 1985 (1985 farm bill, P.L. 99-198), which established the first conservation programs designed to deal with environmental issues resulting from agricultural activities.

Provisions enacted in subsequent farm bills, including in 1990, 1996, 2002, 2008, and 2014,[1] reflect a rapid evolution of the conservation agenda, including the growing influence of environmentalists and other non-agricultural interests in the formulation of conservation policy, and a recognition that agriculture was not treated like other business sectors in many environmental laws.[2] Congress also began funding many of these new programs through mandatory spending for the first time, using the borrowing authority of USDA's Commodity Credit Corporation (CCC)[3] as the funding mechanism instead of annual appropriations. In addition to the original soil erosion and water quality and quantity issues, the conservation agenda has continued to expand to address other natural resource concerns, such as wildlife habitat, air quality, wetlands restoration and protection, energy efficiency, and sustainable agriculture.

Lead agricultural conservation agencies within USDA are the Natural Resources Conservation Service (NRCS), which provides technical assistance and administers most conservation programs, and the Farm Service Agency (FSA), which administers the largest program, the Conservation Reserve Program (CRP). These agencies are supported by others in USDA that supply research and educational assistance, including the Agricultural Research Service (ARS), the Economic Research Service (ERS), the National Institute of Food and Agriculture (NIFA) and the Forest Service (FS).[4] In addition, the conservation effort involves a large array of partners, including other federal agencies, state and local governments, and private organizations, among others, who provide funds, expertise, and other forms of assistance to the agricultural conservation effort.

---

[1] Conservation and Trade Act of 1990 (P.L. 101-624), Federal Agricultural Improvement and Reform Act of 1996 (P.L. 104-127), Farm Security and Rural Investment Act of 2002 (P.L. 107-171), Food, Conservation, and Energy Act of 2008 (P.L. 110-246), and Agricultural Act of 2014 (P.L. 113-79).

[2] For additional discussion on conservation in the farm bill, see CRS Report R43504, *Conservation Provisions in the 2014 Farm Bill (P.L. 113-79)*.

[3] The CCC is the funding mechanism for the mandatory payments that are administered by various agencies of USDA, including all of the farm commodity price and income support programs.

[4] For more information on: ARS projects, see http://www.ars.usda.gov/Research/Research htm; ERS projects, see http://www.ers.usda.gov/topics/natural-resources-environment.aspx#.U-Dy-LE1Ot8; NIFA programs, see http://www.nifa.usda.gov/nea/nre/nre.cfm, and FS projects, see http://www.fs.fed.us/projects/.

Overview

USDA provides technical and financial assistance to attract interest and encourage participation in conservation programs. Participation in all USDA conservation programs is voluntary. These programs protect soil, water, wildlife, and other natural resources on privately owned agricultural lands to limit environmental impacts of production activities both on and off the farm, while maintaining or improving production of food and fiber. Some of these programs center on improving or restoring resources that have been degraded, while others create conditions to limit degradation in the future.

Though programs in this report are listed alphabetically, agricultural conservation programs can be grouped into the following categories based on similarities: working land programs, land retirement and easement programs, watershed programs, emergency programs,[5] compliance,[6] technical assistance, and other programs and overarching provisions.

USDA Agricultural Conservation Programs

Working Lands Programs—typically classified as programs that allow private land to remain in production, while implementing various conservation practices to address natural resource concerns specific to the area.

- Environmental Quality Incentives Program (EQIP), Conservation Stewardship Program (CSP), and Agricultural Management Assistance (AMA).

Land Retirement and Easement Programs—land retirement programs provide federal payments to private agricultural landowners for *temporary* changes in land use or management to achieve environmental benefits. Conversely, conservation easements impose a *permanent* or *long-term* land-use restriction that is voluntarily placed on the land in exchange for a government payment.

- Conservation Reserve Program (includes the Conservation Reserve Enhancement Program (CREP) and Farmable Wetland Program), Agricultural Conservation Easement Program (including agricultural land easements and wetland reserve easements), and Healthy Forests Reserve Program (HFRP).

Watershed Programs—NRCS partners with local sponsors to carry out activities for soil conservation; flood prevention; conservation, development, utilization, and disposal of water; watershed surveys; and dam rehabilitation.

- Watershed and Flood Prevention Operations (also referred to as the Small Watershed Program or P.L. 566 and P.L. 534) and Watershed Rehabilitation program.

Emergency Programs—provide disaster assistance for farmland rehabilitation and impairments to watersheds. Programs are usually funded through supplemental appropriation acts.

- Emergency Conservation Program (ECP), Emergency Forest Restoration Program (EFRP), and Emergency Watershed Protection (EWP) program (includes floodplain easements).

Compliance—prohibits a producer from receiving many federal farm program benefits (including conservation assistance and crop insurance) when conservation program requirements for highly erodible lands and wetlands are not met.

- Highly erodible land conservation (Sodbuster), wetland conservation (Swampbuster), and Sodsaver.

Technical Assistance Programs—provides landowners with science-based conservation information and technical expertise (e.g., engineering and biological) unique to the region and land use type. Usually does not include financial assistance.

- Conservation Operations (includes Conservation Technical Assistance, Soil Survey, Snow Survey and Water Supply Forecasting, and Plant Materials Centers).

Other Conservation Programs and Provisions—Conservation Innovation Grants, Grassroots Source Water Protection Program, Regional Conservation Partnership Program (RCPP), Voluntary Public Access and Habitat Incentive Program, and Water Bank Program.

---

[5] Additional information on emergency land rehabilitation programs may be found in CRS Report R42854, *Emergency Assistance for Agricultural Land Rehabilitation.*

[6] Compliance refers to a series of farm bill provisions that require a minimum level of conservation on environmentally sensitive land in exchange for access to other USDA program benefits. Compliance provisions are not discussed in this report. Additional analysis may be found in CRS Report R42459, *Conservation Compliance and U.S. Farm Policy.*

The majority of conservation programs are funded through USDA's Commodity Credit Corporation (CCC) as mandatory spending. Congress authorizes mandatory programs at specified funding levels (or acreage enrollment levels for the Conservation Reserve and Conservation Stewardship) for multiple years, typically through omnibus legislation such as the farm bill. Mandatory programs are funded at these levels unless Congress limits funding to a lower amount through the appropriations or legislative process (or puts a ceiling on acreage that can be enrolled). Discretionary programs are funded each year through the annual appropriations process.[7]

Despite a steady increase in mandatory funding authority, many conservation programs have been reduced or capped through annual appropriations acts since FY2003. Many of these spending reductions were at the request of the Administration, including in the FY2015 proposal. The mix of programs and amounts of reduction has varied from year to year. Some programs, such as the CRP, have not been reduced by appropriators in recent years, while others, such as the Environmental Quality Incentives Program (EQIP), have been repeatedly reduced below authorized levels. Overall authorized mandatory funding for conservation programs was reduced by close to $5 billion between FY2005 and FY2014.

Sequestration has also had an effect on conservation programs. Sequestration is a process of automatic, largely across-the-board reductions that permanently cancel mandatory and/or discretionary budget authority to enforce statutory budget goals.[8] The Bipartisan Budget Act of 2013 (P.L. 113-67) raised spending limits to avoid sequestration of discretionary accounts in FY2014 and FY2015, but not mandatory accounts. Therefore most all mandatory conservation programs are subject to sequestration in FY2014 and FY2015.[9] Even with sequestration and appropriations act reductions, total mandatory funding for conservation programs has grown from a total of $3.6 billion in FY2005 to $5.4 billion in FY2014.[10]

---

[7] For additional information on the FY2015 appropriation, see CRS Report R43669, *Agriculture and Related Agencies: FY2015 Appropriations*.

[8] The current requirement for sequestration is in the Budget Control Act of 2011 (BCA; P.L. 112-25). For additional information, see CRS Report R42972, *Sequestration as a Budget Enforcement Process: Frequently Asked Questions*.

[9] The Conservation Reserve Program is statutorily exempt from sequestration (2 U.S.C. 905 (g)(1)(A)). Sequestration reductions in FY2014 were reflected in the Congressional Budget Office (CBO) baseline that was used to write the 2014 farm bill. For more information, see CRS Report R42484, *Budget Issues That Shaped the 2014 Farm Bill*.

[10] For additional information on reductions to mandatory conservation programs, see CRS Report IF00036, *Reductions to Mandatory Agricultural Conservation Programs in Appropriations Law (In Focus)*.

2014 Farm Bill

Before the 1985 farm bill, few conservation programs existed and only two would be considered large by today's standards. Prior to the Agricultural Act of 2014 (P.L. 113-79, 2014 farm bill), there were over 20 distinct conservation programs with annual spending greater than $5 billion. The differences and number of these programs created general confusion about the purpose, participation, and policies of the programs. Discussion about simplifying or consolidating conservation programs to reduce overlap and duplication, and to generate savings, continued for a number of years. The 2014 farm bill contained several program consolidation measures, including the repeal of 12 active and inactive programs, the creation of two new programs, and the merging of two programs into existing ones.[11]

Conservation Programs

The tabular presentation that follows provides basic information covering each of the USDA agricultural conservation programs, including

- administering agency or agencies within USDA;

- brief program description;

- major amendments to the program in the Agricultural Act of 2014 (P.L. 113-79), commonly referred to as the 2014 farm bill;

- national scope and availability, including participation levels and acres enrolled;

- states with the highest level of funds obligated or acres enrolled;

- volume of application backlog or public interest in each program;

- authorized funding levels, whether it is mandatory spending or discretionary appropriations, and any funding restrictions;

- FY2014 funding level provided by the Consolidated Appropriations Act of 2014 (P.L. 113-76) or, if applicable, the Agricultural Act of 2014 (P.L. 113-79), authorized level;

- FY2015 funding level requested by the Administration (sequestration not included);

- FY2015 funding level proposed in the Agriculture, Rural Development, Food and Drug Administration, and Related Agencies Appropriations Act of 2015 (H.R. 4800 and S. 2389), or, if applicable, the authorized level in the Agricultural Act of 2014 (sequestration not included);

- whether program funding is sequestrable in FY2015, and under what category (mandatory, non-defense = 7.3% in FY2015, discretionary accounts are not sequestrable in FY2015);[12]

---

[11] For additional information on the amendments to conservation programs in the 2014 farm bill, see CRS Report R43504, *Conservation Provisions in the 2014 Farm Bill (P.L. 113-79)*.

[12] For additional analysis on the impact of sequestration on agricultural programs, see CRS Report R43669, *Agriculture* (continued...)

- statutory authority, recent amendments, and U.S. Code reference;

- expiration date of program authority unless permanently authorized; and

- program's website link.

Information for the following tables is drawn from agency budget presentations, explanatory notes, and websites; written responses to questions published each year in hearing records of the Agriculture Appropriations Subcommittees of the House and Senate Appropriations Committees; and spending estimates from the Congressional Budget Office. Further information about these programs may be found on the NRCS website at http://www.nrcs.usda.gov and on the "conservation programs" page of the FSA website at http://www.fsa.usda.gov.

(...continued)

and Related Agencies: FY2015 Appropriations.

Agricultural Conservation Easement Program (ACEP)

Administering agency(s)	NRCS
Program description	ACEP provides financial and technical assistance through two types of easements: agricultural land easements that limit non-agricultural uses on productive farm or grass lands, and wetland reserve easements that protect and restore wetlands. Priority enrollment is given to expiring CRP acres.
Major 2014 farm bill amendments	Created in the 2014 farm bill from three repealed programs—Farmland Protection Program, Grassland Reserve Program, and Wetlands Reserve Program. General program provisions are the same across both easement types, including ineligible land; subordination, exchange, modification, and termination procedures; and compliance requirements.
National scope	Available nationwide.
Leading states	Not available (new program).
Backlog/Interest	Not available (new program).
Funding authority	Mandatory. FY2014—$400 million, FY2015—$425 million, FY2016—$450 million, FY2017—$500 million, and FY2018—$250 million.
FY2014 funding	$400 million.
FY2015 Administration request	Full authorized level—$425 million.
FY2015 proposed funding	H.R. 4800: limit of $365 million (authorization reduced by $30 million). S. 2389 is silent, thereby allowing the full authorized level of $425 million.
Sequestrable in FY2015?	Yes (mandatory, non-defense).
Statutory authority	Authorized in subtitle D of Title II (§2301) of the Agricultural Act of 2014 (P.L. 113-79) as §1265 of the Food Security Act of 1985 (P.L. 99-198), as amended. 16 U.S.C. 3865-3865d.
Authorization expires	September 30, 2018
Program website	http://www.nrcs.usda.gov/wps/portal/nrcs/main/national/programs/easements/acep/

Agricultural Management Assistance (AMA)

Administering agency(s)	NRCS (conservation assistance), Agricultural Marketing Service (AMS, organic certification), and Risk Management Agency (RMA, production, price, or revenue risk reduction).
Program description	AMA provides cost-sharing assistance under contracts of 1 to 10 years to producers in 16 specified states where participation in the federal crop insurance program has been historically low. Producers use this assistance to construct or improve water management and irrigation structures, plant trees, control soil erosion, practice integrated pest management, practice organic farming, develop value-added processing, and enter into futures, hedging, or options contracts to reduce production, price, or revenue risk.
Major 2014 farm bill amendments	Both the House- and Senate-passed farm bills (H.R. 2642 and S. 954) included amendments to AMA, but none were adopted in the conference agreement.
National scope	Not available nationwide. Eligible states include CT, DE, HI, MD, MA, ME, NV, NH, NJ, NY, PA, RI, UT, VT, WV, and WY. As of the end of FY2013, 465 contracts were being implemented within these states.
Leading states	States with the most funds obligated (for conservation only) in FY2013 include ME ($500,000), PA ($335,000), and WV ($219,000).
Backlog/Interest	A backlog of 281 applications was pending at the end of FY2013, down from a backlog of 420 applications in FY2012. The FY2013 backlog would enroll more than 8,100 acres at a cost of $4.6 million.
Funding authority	Mandatory. Permanently authorized at $10 million for each fiscal year. Funding is split by law among the three USDA agencies: 50%—NRCS, 10%—AMS, and 40%—RMA.
FY2014 funding	$6.4 million (for conservation).
FY2015 Administration request	Full authorized level—$10 million ($5 million for conservation).
FY2015 proposed funding	H.R. 4800 and S. 2389 are silent, thereby allowing the full authorized level of $10 million ($5 million for conservation).
Sequestrable in FY2015?	Yes (mandatory, non-defense).
Statutory authority	Authorized in Title I, §133 of the Agricultural Risk Protection Act of 2000 (P.L. 106-224) as §524(b) of the Federal Crop Insurance Act, as amended. 7 U.S.C. 1524(b).
Authorization expires	Permanent authorization.
Program website	http://www.nrcs.usda.gov/wps/portal/nrcs/main/national/programs/financial/ama

Conservation Operations (CO)—
Conservation Technical Assistance (CTA)

Administering agency(s)	NRCS.
Program description	Conservation Operations (CO) is the primary account funding technical assistance within NRCS. More than 80% of CO funding is for Conservation Technical Assistance (CTA), which provides conservation planning and implementation assistance through field staff placed in almost all counties within the United States and territories. This assistance is provided to producers and land owners who voluntarily apply natural resource conservation systems, consisting of one or more practices, on private and other non-federal lands. Other components of CO include the Soil Surveys, Snow Survey and Water Supply Forecasting, and Plant Materials Centers.
Major 2014 farm bill amendments	None.
National scope	Available nationwide. CTA was funded at $676 million and 4,691 staff years for FY2013. Total CO spending for FY2013 (after rescissions, transfers, and sequestration) was $831 million and 5,345 staff years.
Leading states	No data are available for the CTA subset in FY2014, but the three leading states for total CO funding (estimate) are TX ($34.9 million), IA ($24.3 million), and KS ($18.7 million).
Backlog/Interest	Not available.
Funding authority	Discretionary. No specific authorization level.
FY2014 funding	$714.2 million for CTA out of $812.9 million appropriated for all CO.
FY2015 Administration request	$716.6 million for CTA out of $814.8 million appropriated for all CO.
FY2015 proposed funding	H.R. 4800: $843 million for CO, including $747 million for CTA. S. 2389: $849 million for CO, CTA is an unspecified subset.
Sequestrable in FY2015?	No (discretionary spending).
Statutory authority	Authorized in the Soil Conservation and Domestic Allotment Act (P.L. 74-46), as amended. 16 U.S.C. 590a-g, 16 U.S.C. 590q.
Authorization expires	Permanent authorization.
Program website	http://www.nrcs.usda.gov/programs/cta/ (CTA); http://www.nrcs.usda.gov/wps/portal/nrcs/site/soils/home/ (soil survey); http://www.wcc.nrcs.usda.gov/ (snow survey and water supply forecasting); and http://plant-materials.nrcs.usda.gov/ (plant materials centers).

Conservation Reserve Program (CRP)

Administering agency(s)	FSA, technical assistance by NRCS.
Program description	CRP provides annual rental payments, usually over 10 years, to producers to replace crops on highly erodible and environmentally sensitive land with long-term resource-conserving plantings. Bids to enroll land are solicited during a limited time period, then compared using an Environmental Benefits Index (EBI). Those with the highest EBI scores are accepted. Imbedded in the CRP are several small and more focused programs that bypass the general bidding process, some established in law and others established administratively, to address specific resource topics, including more concentrated resource problems in a portion of a state, protection of small isolated agricultural wetlands, and improvement of habitat for upland game birds. All lands that qualify for these subprograms are automatically accepted and enrolled on a continuous basis.
Major 2014 farm bill amendments	Reduces enrollment ceiling from 32 million acres to 24 million acres by FY2018; amends emergency harvesting, grazing, and permits other use of forage, in some cases, without a reduction in rental rate; allows a one time, penalty-free, early-out in FY2015 for contracts enrolled longer than five years and containing no environmentally sensitive practices; and incorporates grassland contracts, similar to what was repealed under the Grassland Reserve Program (GRP).
National scope	Available nationwide. In FY2014, following reauthorization in the 2014 farm bill, USDA announced continuous sign-up beginning June 9. In lieu of a general sign-up in FY2014, USDA will offer expiring CRP contracts a one year extension. As of July 2014, there are 672,130 active contracts on 376,544 farms with 25.5 million acres enrolled.
Leading states	Leading states in terms of acres are TX (3.2 million), KS (2.3 million), and CO (2.0 million). Leading states in terms of number of contracts are IA (99,815), IL (78,808), and MN (57,003).
Backlog/Interest	In FY2013, enrollment ended at 26.84 million acres. The expiration of contracts (3.3 million acres) and a delay in reauthorizing the program dropped enrollment to 25.5 million acres by May 2014. An estimated 2 million acres are scheduled to expire at the end of FY2014. Between FY2007 and FY2014, over 17.1 million CRP acres under contact have expired and were not reenrolled in the program.
Funding authority	Mandatory. At any one time, CRP can enroll no more than: 27.5 million acres in FY2014; 26 million acres in FY2015; 25 million acres in FY2016; and 24 million acres in FY2017 and FY2018. No funding amount specified.
FY2014 est. funding	$1.9 billion (based on the estimated number of acres that will be enrolled, including technical assistance).
FY2015 Administration request	Full authorized level—estimated at $2.1 billion (based on the estimated number of acres that will be enrolled, including technical assistance).
FY2015 proposed funding	H.R. 4800 and S. 2389 are silent, thereby allowing the full authorized level of 26 million acres.
Sequestrable in FY2015?	No (statutorily exempt).
Statutory authority	Authorized in §1231-§1235 of the Food Security Act of 1985 (P.L. 99-198), as amended. Amended in §2001-§2008 of the Agricultural Act of 2014 (P.L. 113-79). 16 U.S.C. 3831(a)-3835a.
Authorization expires	September 30, 2018.
Program website	http://www.fsa.usda.gov/FSA/webapp?area=home&subject=copr&topic=crp

CRP—Conservation Reserve Enhancement Program (CREP)

Administering agency(s)	FSA, technical assistance by NRCS.
Program description	This subprogram of CRP partners with states at their request. States propose sub-state areas, such as a watershed, where environmental or resource concerns are more concentrated and can be addressed by enrolling up to 100,000 acres per project. States contribute 20% of the funding so that larger payments can be made, in order to encourage greater participation. Sign-up is held on a continuous basis.
Major 2014 farm bill amendments	None.
National scope	There are 45 CREP agreements in 33 states, including 73,198 contracts on 48,431 farms, enrolling a total of 1.3 million acres, as of July 2014.
Leading states	Leading states in terms of acres enrolled are PA (164,201), IL (140,998), and OH (115,393). States leading in number of contracts are OH (13,962), PA (9,755), and IL (7,659).
Backlog/Interest	Not applicable since any eligible land can be enrolled at any time; participation has been much higher in some states than in others, but that is due, reportedly, to how the program is promoted. Average rental payments are higher than for acreage under the general CRP sign-up process.
Funding authority	Unspecified acreage subset of CRP.
FY2014 funding	Unspecified acreage subset of CRP.
FY2015 Administration request	Unspecified acreage subset of CRP.
FY2015 proposed funding	Unspecified acreage subset of CRP.
Sequestrable in FY2015?	No (statutorily exempt).
Statutory authority	Authority derived from CRP statutory authority (see "Conservation Reserve Program (CRP)").
Authorization expires	September 30, 2018.
Program website	http://www.fsa.usda.gov/FSA/webapp?area=home&subject=copr&topic=cep

CRP—Farmable Wetland Program

Administering agency(s)	FSA, technical assistance by NRCS.
Program description	This 750,000 acre subprogram of the CRP enrolls small isolated agricultural wetlands. On a single tract of land, enrollment is set at a maximum of 40 contiguous wetland acres. "Flooded farmland" has a 20-acre limit. Eligible lands include wetlands that were cropped 3 of the preceding 10 years, and buffers sufficient to protect them, on which the hydrology will be restored and a vegetative cover established. Sign-up is held on a continuous basis.
Major 2014 farm bill amendments	Renames the pilot program "Farmable Wetland Program." Reauthorizes the program through FY2018, and clarifies language related to constructed wetlands receiving water from agricultural drainage. Reduces acreage limitation from 1 million acres to 750,000 acres.
National scope	Active contracts in 23 participating states, including AL, AR, CO, ID, IL, IN, IA, KS, LA, MD, MI, MN, MS, MO, MT, NE, NC, ND, OH, OK, SD, WA and WI. As of July 2014, there are 15,549 contracts on 12,071 farms for a total of 339,673 enrolled acres.
Leading states	In terms of acres, the leading states are ND (95,938 acres), SD (90,715 acres), and IA (76,832 acres). The largest number of contracts are in IA (4,915), followed by SD (4,071) and MN (3,360).
Backlog/Interest	Not applicable since any eligible land can be enrolled at any time; participation has been much higher in some states than in others, but that is due, reportedly, to how the program is promoted and the amount of eligible land with a state.
Funding authority	Mandatory. No more than 750,000 acres enrolled at any one time and no more than 100,000 acres in any state (may be increased to 200,000 acres after agency review).
FY2014 funding	Unspecified acreage subset of CRP.
FY2015 Administration request	Unspecified acreage subset of CRP.
FY2015 proposed funding	Unspecified acreage subset of CRP.
Sequestrable in FY2015?	No (statutorily exempt).
Statutory authority	Authorized in Title XI of Agriculture and Related Agency appropriations, 2001 (P.L. 106-387) as §1231B of the Food Security Act of 1985 (P.L. 99-198), as amended. Amended by §2002 of the Agricultural Act of 2014 (P.L. 113-79). 16 U.S.C. 3831b.
Authorization expires	September 30, 2018.
Program website	http://www.fsa.usda.gov/FSA/webapp?area=home&subject=copr&topic=fwp

Conservation Stewardship Program (CSP)

Administering agency(s)	NRCS
Program description	CSP provides financial and technical assistance to promote the conservation and improvement of soil, water, air, energy, plant and animal life, and other conservation purposes on tribal and private working lands. Contracts (five years in length with the option of extension) are based on meeting or exceeding a "stewardship threshold." Payments are based on the actual costs of installing conservation measures, any foregone income, and the value of the expected environmental outcomes. Enrollment is offered through a continuous sign-up and applications are accepted year-round.
Major 2014 farm bill amendments	Reduces the enrollment cap from 12.769 million acres annually to 10 million acres annually. Reorganizes the statutory language and refocuses the program on generating additional conservation benefits. Raises the entry bar for participants to two priority resource concerns upon entry and meet or exceed one additional priority resource concern by the end of the contract. Contract renewal participants must meet the threshold for two additional priority resources concerns or exceed the threshold for two existing priority resource concerns. Removes the 10% limitation on nonindustrial private forest land and provides flexible transition options for land coming out of CRP.
National scope	Available nationwide. The program held its first sign-up in 2009, and at the end of FY2013, had over 60 million acres enrolled.
Leading states	In FY2013, NM had the most total acres funded (995,483), followed by SD (984,966) and TX (899,768). The most funding obligated in FY2013 was in AR ($17.8 million), SD ($11.1 million), and ND ($10.7 million).
Backlog/Interest	In FY2012, CSP provided $168 million in funding to treat 12,109,876 acres. 2,876 applications went unfunded, covering an estimated 4,193,654 acres, worth approximately $52.7 million.
Funding authority	Mandatory. 10 million acres each fiscal year. No funding amount specified.
FY2014 est. funding	$1.079 billion (based on the estimated number of acres that will be enrolled, including technical assistance).
FY2015 Administration request	Full authorized level—estimated at $1.4 billion (based on the estimated number of acres that will be enrolled, including technical assistance).
FY2015 proposed funding	H.R. 4800: limit of $1.16 billion, unknown impact to acres. S. 2389 is silent, thereby allowing the full authorized level of 10 million acres.
Sequestrable in FY2015?	Yes (mandatory, non-defense).
Statutory authority	Authorized in §2301 of the Food, Conservation, and Energy Act of 2008 (P.L. 110-246) as §1238D-§1238G of the Food Security Act of 1985 (P.L. 99-198), as amended. Amended in §2101 of the Agricultural Act of 2014 (P.L. 113-79). 16 U.S.C. 3838h-3838n.
Authorization expires	September 30, 2018.
Program website	http://www.nrcs.usda.gov/wps/portal/nrcs/main/national/programs/financial/csp

Emergency Conservation Program (ECP)

Administering agency(s)	FSA, technical assistance by NRCS.
Program description	ECP provides emergency funding and technical assistance to producers to rehabilitate farmland damaged by natural disasters (e.g., hurricanes, floods, wind, and erosion) through activities such as removing debris, and implementing emergency water conservation measures in response to severe droughts.
Major 2014 farm bill amendments	None.
National scope	Available nationwide. Participation varies widely and unpredictably from year to year. The last funding received was in FY2013. The Disaster Relief Appropriations Act of 2013 (P.L. 113-2) provided $15 million to be used for necessary expenses related to the consequences of Hurricane Sandy and major disasters declared pursuant to the Stafford Act (42 U.S.C. 5121 et seq.) only, and the Consolidated and Further Continuing Appropriations Act of 2013 (P.L. 113-6) provided an additional $10.8 million.
Leading states	Not applicable.
Backlog/Interest	Not applicable.
Funding authority	Discretionary. No specific authorization level.
FY2014 funding	$0
FY2015 Administration request to date	$0
FY2015 proposed funding to date	H.R. 4800: $0. S. 2389: $11.755 million.
Sequestrable in FY2015?	No (discretionary spending).
Statutory authority	Authorized in §401 of the Agriculture Credit Act of 1978 (P.L. 95-334), as amended. 16 U.S.C. 2201-2205.
Authorization expires	Permanent authorization.
Program website	http://www.fsa.usda.gov/FSA/webapp?area=home&subject=copr&topic=ecp

Emergency Forest Restoration Program (EFRP)

Administering agency(s)	FSA, technical assistance by NRCS.
Program description	EFRP provides cost-share assistance to private forestland owners to repair and rehabilitate damage caused by a natural disaster on nonindustrial private forest land. Natural disasters include wildfires, hurricanes or excessive winds, drought, ice storms or blizzards, floods, or other resource-impacting events, as determined by USDA.
Major 2014 farm bill amendments	None.
National scope	Available nationwide. Participation varies widely and unpredictably from year to year. The last funding received was in FY2013. The Disaster Relief Appropriations Act of 2013 (P.L. 113-2) provided $23 million to be used for necessary expenses related to the consequences of Hurricane Sandy and major disasters declared pursuant to the Stafford Act (42 U.S.C. 5121 et seq.) only, and the Consolidated and Further Continuing Appropriations Act of 2013 (P.L. 113-6) provided an additional $13.8 million.
Leading states	Not applicable.
Backlog/Interest	Not applicable.
Funding authority	Discretionary. No specific authorization level.
FY2014 funding	$0
FY2015 Administration request to date	$0
FY2015 proposed funding to date	H.R. 4800: $0. S. 2389: $15 million to be made available for necessary expenses resulting from a major disaster declared pursuant to the Stafford Act.
Sequestrable in FY2015?	No (discretionary spending).
Statutory authority	Authorized in §8203 of the Food, Conservation, and Energy Act of 2008 (P.L. 110-246) as §407 of the Agriculture Credit Act of 1978 (P.L. 95-334). 16 U.S.C. 2206.
Authorization expires	Permanent authorization.
Program website	http://www.fsa.usda.gov/FSA/webapp?area=home&subject=copr&topic=ecp

Emergency Watershed Protection (EWP)

Administering agency(s)	NRCS on private lands, U.S. Forest Service on National Forest Systems lands.
Program description	EWP provides technical and financial assistance to reduce hazards to life and property in watersheds that have been damaged by natural disasters. Assistance includes disaster cleanup and recovery activities, and purchasing easements in floodplains that will benefit natural resources such as wetlands, while reducing the risk of exposure to future natural disasters.
Major 2014 farm bill amendments	Authorizes USDA to modify and terminate floodplain easements provided the current landowner agrees, and the modification or termination addresses a compelling public need for which there is no practical alternative, and is in the public interest.
National scope	Available nationwide. Participation varies widely and unpredictably from year to year. The last funding received was in FY2013. The Disaster Relief Appropriations Act of 2013 (P.L. 113-2) provided $180 million to be used for necessary expenses related to the consequences of Hurricane Sandy and major disasters declared pursuant to the Stafford Act (42 U.S.C. 5121 et seq.) only, and the Consolidated and Further Continuing Appropriations Act of 2013 (P.L. 113-6) provided an additional $63.7 million (including $48.2 million for major disasters declared pursuant to the Stafford Act).
Leading states	Not applicable.
Backlog/Interest	Not applicable.
Funding authority	Discretionary. No specific authorization level.
FY2014 funding	$0
FY2015 Administration request to date	$0
FY2015 proposed funding to date	H.R. 4800: $0. S. 2389: $109.978 million, including $85 million which must be made available for necessary expenses resulting from a major disaster declared pursuant to the Stafford Act.
Sequestrable in FY2015?	No (discretionary spending).
Statutory authority	Authorized in §216 of P.L. 81-516 and §403 of the Agriculture Credit Act of 1978 (P.L. 95-334), as amended. Amended in §2506 of the Agricultural Act of 2014 (P.L. 113-79). 16 U.S.C. 2203; and 33 U.S.C. 701b-1.
Authorization expires	Permanent authorization.
Program website	http://www.nrcs.usda.gov/wps/portal/nrcs/main/national/programs/landscape/ewpp

Environmental Quality Incentives Program (EQIP)

Administering agency(s)	NRCS
Program description	EQIP provides financial and technical assistance to producers and land owners to plan and install structural, vegetative, and land management practices on eligible lands to alleviate natural resource problems. Eligible producers enter into contracts to receive payment for implementing conservation practices. Approved activities are carried out according to an EQIP plan developed in conjunction with the producer that identifies the appropriate conservation practice(s) to address resource concerns on the land. Sixty percent of the funds are targeted to practices benefiting livestock.
Major 2014 farm bill amendments	Incorporates the Wildlife Habitat Incentives Program (WHIP) into EQIP with a 5% allocation to wildlife habitat practices; removes the minimum one-year contract length requirement; adds veteran farmer or rancher to the list of certain producers eligible for cost-share rates up to 90% and advanced payments; raises the payment limit to an aggregate of $450,000 between FY2014-FY2018 and eliminates the waiver authority for contracts of environmental significance; repeals the Agricultural Water Enhancement Program (AWEP); reauthorizes the innovative grants program (see "EQIP—Conservation Innovation Grants (CIG)"); retains the allocation of 60% of funding each year to practices related to livestock production; and reauthorizes and reduces the air quality funding carve-out from $37.5 million to $25 million annually.
National scope	Available nationwide. In FY2013, EQIP obligated over $989 million for 44,823 contracts covering 13.8 million acres.
Leading states	In FY2013, the top three states by contracts signed were TX (4,536), AR (2,786), and MS (2,269). The most funding obligated was in TX ($119 million), CA ($97 million), and AR ($72 million).
Backlog/Interest	In FY2013, 44,825 applications were funded (45.7%) and 53,319 applications went unfunded. The total estimated cost of this backlog is $1.2 billion. The most unfunded applications were submitted in AR (5,960), OK (3,486), and MO (2,532).
Funding authority	Mandatory. FY2014—$1.35 billion, FY2015—$1.6 billion, FY2016—$1.65 billion, FY2017—$1.65 billion, and FY2018—$1.75 billion.
FY2014 funding	$1.35 billion.
FY2015 Administration request	$1.35 billion (authorization reduced by $136 million).
FY2015 proposed funding	H.R. 4800: $1.391 billion (authorization reduced by $95 million). S. 2389: $1.35 billion (authorization reduced by $136 million).
Sequestrable in FY2015?	Yes (mandatory, non-defense).
Statutory authority	Authorized in subtitle D of Title III (§331-336) of the Federal Agriculture Improvement and Reform Act of 1996 (P.L. 104-127) as §1240-§12401 of the Food Security Act of 1985 (P.L. 99-198), as amended. Amended by §2201-§2206 of the Agricultural Act of 2014 (P.L. 113-79). 16 U.S.C. 3839aa-3839aa9.
Authorization expires	September 30, 2018.
Program website	http://www.nrcs.usda.gov/wps/portal/nrcs/main/national/programs/financial/eqip

EQIP—Conservation Innovation Grants (CIG)

Administering agency(s)	NRCS
Program description	CIG is a subprogram of EQIP that awards competitive grants to state and local agencies, non-governmental organizations, tribes, and individuals to implement innovative conservation techniques and practices. Annual requests for proposals are posted on http://www.grants.gov and include separate funding categories for national and state level competitions. Examples of eligible projects include market systems for pollution reduction, demonstrating precision agriculture, capturing nutrients through a community anaerobic digester, and establishing a tribal partnership for regional habitat conservation.
Major 2014 farm bill amendments	Adds research and demonstration activities, and new technology pilot testing as eligible projects; reauthorizes but reduces the air quality funding carve-out to $25 million of EQIP annually through FY2018; and adds a reporting requirement that no later than December 31, 2014, and every two years thereafter, a report must be submitted to Congress regarding CIG funding, project results, and technology transfer efforts.
National scope	Available nationwide with select states offering state competitions. In FY2013, CIG awarded a total of $24.1 million through two national CIG competitions. The first competition ($18.7 million, 46 projects) focused on nutrient management, economics, energy, soil health, wildlife. The second competition ($5.4 million, 13 projects) focused on adaptation to drought.
Leading states	None identified.
Backlog/Interest	None identified.
Funding authority	Unspecified subset of EQIP.
FY2014 funding	Up to $15 million available for the national competition. Application deadline closed May 5, 2014. Unknown amount available for state competitions.
FY2015 Administration request	Unspecified subset of EQIP.
FY2015 proposed funding	Unspecified subset of EQIP.
Sequestrable in FY2015?	Yes, as a subset of EQIP.
Statutory authority	Authorized in §2301 of the Farm Security and Rural Investment Act of 2002 (P.L. 107-171) as §1240H of the Food Security Act of 1985 (P.L. 99-198), as amended. Amended by §2207 of the Agricultural Act of 2014 (P.L. 113-79). 16 U.S.C. 3839aa-8.
Authorization expires	September 30, 2018.
Program website	http://www.nrcs.usda.gov/wps/portal/nrcs/main/national/programs/financial/cig

Grassroots Source Water Protection Program

Administering agency(s)	FSA
Program description	Grassroots Source Water Protection Program provides funding to the National Rural Water Association for technical assistance to operate state's source water protection program. Local programs encourage the voluntary adoption of practices that prevent drinking water pollution.
Major 2014 farm bill amendments	Reauthorizes discretionary funding authority and authorizes $5 million in mandatory funding to remain available until expended.
National scope	In September 2013, the program was expanded to all 50 states.
Leading states	Annual appropriations are divided equally among all states.
Backlog/Interest	None identified.
Funding authority	Mandatory: FY2014—$5 million (to remain available until expended). Discretionary: $20 million annually.
FY2014 funding	$5.5 million in discretionary funding and $5 million in mandatory funding.
FY2015 Administration request	$0
FY2015 proposed funding	H.R. 4800: $2.5 million. S. 2389: $6.5 million.
Sequestrable in FY2015?	No (discretionary spending).
Statutory authority	Authorized in §2502 of the Farm Security and Rural Investment Act of 2002 (P.L. 107-171) as §1240O of the Food Security Act of 1985 (P.L. 99-198), as amended. Amended by §2502 of the Agricultural Act of 2014 (P.L. 113-79). 16 U.S.C. 3839bb-2
Authorization expires	September, 30, 2018
Program website	http://www.nrcs.usda.gov/wps/portal/nrcs/detail/national/programs/farmbill/?cid=stelprdb1242739

Healthy Forests Reserve Program (HFRP)

Administering agency(s)	NRCS
Program description	HFRP assists landowners in restoring and enhancing forest ecosystems using 10-year agreements, 30-year contracts, 30-year easements, and permanent easements.
Major 2014 farm bill amendments	Eliminates mandatory funding authority and replaces with an authorization to receive appropriations. Adds a definition of "acreage owned by Indian tribes." Provides flexibility for funding technical assistance.
National scope	Not available nationwide. Limited participation in CA, GA, IN, KY, ME, MI, MS, OH, OK, OR, PA, and SC.
Leading states	In FY2013, the program enrolled 18 permanent easements, one 30-year easement, and two 10-year agreements for a total of 8,486 acres. In FY2013, states with the most funding obligated were OR ($1.8 million), KY ($1.2 million), and MS ($705,000).
Backlog/Interest	During FY2013, a total of 38 applications were submitted and 21 applications were enrolled (55%).
Funding authority	Discretionary. $12 million annually.
FY2014 funding	$6.4 million.
FY2015 Administration request	$0
FY2015 proposed funding	$0
Sequestrable in FY2015?	No (discretionary spending).
Statutory authority	Authorized in Title V Healthy Forest Restoration Act of 2003 (P.L. 108-148), as amended. Amended by §8203 of the Agricultural Act of 2014 (P.L. 113-79). 16 U.S.C. 6572.
Authorization expires	September 30, 2018.
Program website	http://www.nrcs.usda.gov/wps/portal/nrcs/main/national/programs/easements/forests

Regional Conservation Partnership Program (RCPP)

Administering agency(s)	NRCS
Program description	RCPP provides financial and technical assistance for multi-state or watershed-scale projects. The program creates partnership opportunities to target and leverage federal conservation funding for specific areas and resource concerns. Project areas are defined by eligible partners and are selected through a competitive state or national competition. Partnership agreements are for five years with a possible one-year extension. In addition to defining the project area, providing assistance, and possibly acting on behalf of the producers within the project area, partners must also provide a "significant portion" of the overall cost of the project. Funds are also directed through "critical conservation areas" (CCA) selected by NRCS. In FY2014, CCAs include Chesapeake Bay Watershed, Great Lakes Region, Mississippi River Basin, Colorado River Basin, Longleaf Pine Range, Columbia River Basin, Prairie Grasslands Region, and California Bay Delta. Funding is statutorily divided as: critical conservation areas—35%, national projects—40%, and state projects—25%.
Major 2014 farm bill amendments	Created in the 2014 farm bill from four repealed programs—Agricultural Water Enhancement Program, the Cooperative Conservation Partnership Initiative, the Chesapeake Bay Watershed Program, and the Great Lakes Basin Program for soil erosion and sediment control. RCPP contracts follow the existing rules and requirements of the covered programs.
National scope	To be eligible for an RCPP contract, a producer must be located in either a CCA or a selected partnership area, but is not required to work with the sponsoring project partner and may choose to work directly with NRCS. Partnership applications are accepted in two phases: pre-proposal and full proposal. In FY2014, 230 pre-proposal applicants were invited to submit a full proposal.
Leading states	In FY2014, following the pre-proposal process the three funding categories received the following (most received): state projects—278 proposals (CA—19 proposals), CCA—202 proposals (Mississippi River Basin—61 proposals), and national projects—60 proposals.
Backlog/Interest	In FY2014, the total amount of funding requested was more than six times the amount available. During the pre-proposal round, 600 proposals were received requesting about $2.8 billion. These included close to 5,000 partners willing to match $3 billion of their own funding.
Funding authority	Mandatory. 7% of available covered conservation program funds (EQIP, CSP, ACEP, and HFRP) plus an additional $100 million annually.
FY2014 est. funding	$394 million.
FY2015 Administration request	Full authorized level.
FY2015 proposed funding	H.R. 4800 and S. 2389 are silent, thereby allowing the full authorized level.
Sequestrable in FY2015?	Yes (mandatory, non-defense).
Statutory authority	Authorized in subtitle E of Title II (§2401) of the Agricultural Act of 2014 (P.L. 113-79) as §1271 of the Food Security Act of 1985 (P.L. 99-198), as amended. 16 U.S.C. 3871-3871f.
Authorization expires	September 30, 2018.
Program website	http://www.nrcs.usda.gov/wps/portal/nrcs/main/national/programs/farmbill/rcpp/

Voluntary Public Access and Habitat Incentive Program

Administering agency(s)	NRCS
Program description	The Voluntary Public Access and Habitat Incentive Program encourages owners and operators of privately held farm, ranch, and forest land to voluntarily make that land available for access by the public for wildlife-dependent recreation, including hunting or fishing, under programs implemented by state or tribal governments. Competitive grants are offered to states and tribal governments for expanding existing access programs or creating new programs. Grants are reduced by 25% if opening dates for migratory bird hunting in a state are not consistent for residents and nonresidents.
Major 2014 farm bill amendments	Reduces and extends authorization of mandatory funding. Requires USDA to submit a report to Congress no later than 2016 on the effectiveness of the program.
National scope	Available nationwide. 26 states and one tribal government have participated to date. In FY2014, nine states and one Tribal Nation received grants for a total of $20 million.
Leading states	In FY2014, states receiving the most funding were PA ($6 million), IA ($3 million), and TX ($2.2 million).
Backlog/Interest	None identified.
Funding authority	Mandatory. $40 million in total for the period of FY2014-FY2018.
FY2014 est. funding	$20 million.
FY2015 Administration request	Full authorized level.
FY2015 proposed funding	H.R. 4800 and S. 2389 are silent, thereby allowing the full authorized level of $40 million between FY2014 and FY2018.
Sequestrable in FY2015?	Yes (mandatory, non-defense).
Statutory authority	Authorized in Title II, §2606 of the Food, Conservation, and Energy Act of 2008 (P.L. 110-246) as §1240R of the Food Security Act of 1985 (P.L. 99-198), as amended. Amended by §2503 of the Agricultural Act of 2014 (P.L. 113-79). 16 U.S.C. 3839bb-5.
Authorization expires	September 30, 2018.
Program website	http://www.nrcs.usda.gov/wps/portal/nrcs/detail/national/programs/farmbill/?cid=stelprdb1242739

Water Bank Program

Administering agency(s)	NRCS
Program description	The Water Bank Program offers 10-year, non-renewable rental agreements to landowners to maintain wetlands in lieu of draining the land for agricultural production. No financial assistance is offered for conservation practices. Applications are ranked based on land use type and flooding impact. Payment rates are as follows: $50/acre/year for cropland, $35/acre/year for pasture and range land (grazing lands), and $20/acre/year for forestland. The program was authorized in 1970 and operated until funding was eliminated in 1994 in favor of longer-term conservation programs. After 17 years of no funding, the program was appropriated $7.5 million in FY2012. These funds were obligated exclusively in Minnesota, North Dakota, and South Dakota and were focused on flood reduction.
Major 2014 farm bill amendments	None.
National scope	Not available nationwide. Eligible states include MN, ND, and SD.
Leading states	In FY2012, (most recent data available) eligible states receiving the most funding were ND ($6.4 million), SD ($994,000), and MN ($45,000).
Backlog/Interest	NRCS reports that in FY2012, $7 million was obligated for 107 rental agreements covering 15,945 acres. There was a backlog of 523 applications with an estimated value of $28.9 million covering 70,631 acre in the three eligible states.
Funding authority	Discretionary. No specific authorization level.
FY2014 funding	$4 million.
FY2015 Administration request	$0
FY2015 proposed funding	H.R. 4800: $0. S. 2389: $4 million.
Sequestrable in FY2015?	No (discretionary spending).
Statutory authority	Authorized in the Water Bank Act (P.L. 91-559), as amended. 16 U.S.C. 1301-1311.
Authorization expires	Permanent authorization.
Program website	http://www.nrcs.usda.gov/wps/portal/nrcs/detail/national/programs/financial/?&cid=stelprdb1047790

Watershed and Flood Prevention Operations

Administering agency(s)	NRCS
Program description	Also referred to as the Small Watershed Program, Watershed and Flood Prevention Operations are two separate authorizations under which more than 11,000 structures have been built in more than 1,700 active and completed projects. The P.L. 78-534 Flood Prevention Operations Program authorizes 11 projects, while the P.L. 83-566 Small Watershed Operations Program authorizes watershed projects generally. Projects may be authorized for any of eight purposes; almost all projects have flood control as an authorized purpose. Under P.L. 566, NRCS provides technical and financial assistance to plan and install projects on private lands, in cooperation with local sponsors, states, and other public agencies. The small watershed project costs are shared with local partners. Projects are limited to a maximum size, including 25,000 acre-feet of total capacity and 250,000 acres in extent. Projects above a specified size require congressional committee authorization.
Major 2014 farm bill amendments	None.
National scope	Available nationwide. A total of 439 work plans are complete under P.L. 534, and 1,380 are active or completed under P.L. 566.
Leading states	None identified.
Backlog/Interest	An estimated $921 million is needed to install the remaining measures in the 302 active watershed projects. States with the greatest value of unfunded commitments are TX ($245 million), OK ($126 million), and MO ($111 million).
Funding authority	Discretionary. No specific authorization level.
FY2014 funding	$0 appropriated. $3 million congressionally directed from Conservation Operations (CO).
FY2015 Administration request	$0
FY2015 proposed funding	H.R. 4800: $0. S. 2389: $0, but congressionally directs $5.6 million from CO.
Sequestrable in FY2015?	No (discretionary spending).
Statutory authority	Authorized in the Flood Control Act of 1944 (P.L. 78-534), as amended, and the Watershed Protection and Flood Prevention Act (P.L. 83-566), as amended. 33 U.S.C. 701b-1 and 16 U.S.C. 1000 et. seq.
Authorization expires	Permanent authorization.
Program website	http://www.nrcs.usda.gov/wps/portal/nrcs/detailfull/national/programs/landscape/?&cid=nrcs143_008271

Watershed Rehabilitation Program

Administering agency(s)	NRCS
Program description	The Watershed Rehabilitation Program provides technical and financial assistance for planning, design, and implementation to rehabilitate aging watershed dam projects (including upgrading or removing dams) in communities to address health and safety concerns. Only dams constructed under the Watershed and Flood Prevention Operations program are eligible. Small watershed project dams have a 50-year design life, and 3,224 reached or exceeded that time span by the end of 2013. By the end of 2016, this number will be 4,749.
Major 2014 farm bill amendments	Reauthorizes both mandatory and discretionary funding authority.
National scope	Only available for dams built through the Watershed and Flood Prevention Operations program and the Resource Conservation and Development (RC&D) program. A total of 268 rehabilitation projects have been funded in 30 states between FY2000 and FY2013. A total of 127 projects are complete with 141 awaiting funding and implementation.
Leading states	States with the largest number of dam projects funded over the life of the program (2000-2013) are OK (50), MS (24), and GA (24). States with the highest allocation in FY2014 were AZ ($98.1 million), TX ($33.8 million), and OK ($26.4 million).
Backlog/Interest	In FY2014, over $900 million in requests were received from public sponsors. As of June 2014, NRCS expects approximately $336 million in requests to remain unfunded at the end of the fiscal year.
Funding authority	Mandatory: FY2014—$250 million (to remain available until expended). Discretionary: FY2008-FY2018—$85 million annually.
FY2014 funding	$12 million in discretionary funding and $250 in mandatory funding (authorization reduced by $153 million).
FY2015 Administration request	$0 in discretionary funding and $0 in mandatory funding (authorization reduced by permanently cancelling the remaining $142 million of annual carry-over).
FY2015 proposed funding	H.R. 4800: $25 in discretionary funding and $92 million in mandatory funding (authorization reduced by $50 million). S. 2389: $0 in discretionary funding and $0 in mandatory funding (authorization reduced by $142 million).
Sequestrable in FY2015?	Yes (mandatory, non-defense) and no (discretionary spending).
Statutory authority	Authorized in §313 of the Grain Standards and Warehouse Improvement Act of 2000 (P.L. 106-472) as §14 of the Watershed Protection and Flood Prevention Act, as amended. Amended by §2505 of the Agricultural Act of 2014 (P.L. 113-79). 16 U.S.C. 1012.
Authorization expires	September 30, 2018.
Program website	http://www.nrcs.usda.gov/wps/portal/nrcs/main/national/programs/landscape/wr

Author Contact Information

Megan Stubbs
Specialist in Agricultural Conservation and Natural
Resources Policy
mstubbs@crs.loc.gov, 7-8707